Walk Humbly

*Encouragements for
Living, Working, and Being*

Samuel Wells

William B. Eerdmans Publishing Company
Grand Rapids, Michigan

Wm. B. Eerdmans Publishing Co.
4035 Park East Court SE, Grand Rapids, Michigan 49546
www.eerdmans.com

25 24 23 22 21 20 19   1 2 3 4 5 6 7

ISBN 978-0-8028-7696-6

Library of Congress Cataloging-in-Publication Data

A catalog record for this book is available from the Library of Congress.

For Andrew and Frances

Contents

Preface

This is a short book: but it may not turn out to be a quick read. It's designed to be pondered, weighed, tasted, and digested one chapter at a time—maybe one paragraph at a time, perhaps even one sentence at a time. If you find it a little dense, perhaps you're seeking to read it a little too fast. Its reading demands of the reader what its argument asks: humility, gentleness, patience, gratitude.

It is shaped to move, inspire, encourage, persuade, challenge. What it commends is first a way of seeing and inhabiting existence; but second, a way of living, relating, and seeking. It's based around a single idea; but it doesn't promote simply an idea: it isn't shy of describing the implications of that idea. Those implications might be called essential existence.

In 1927 the American writer and lawyer Max Ehr-mann wrote a prose poem, beginning with the words "Go placidly," that he published in 1948. It achieved fame, after his death, under the title "Desiderata." The rector of St. Paul's Church, Baltimore, included it in an anthology in 1956, and an urban myth grew that suggested it had been composed in the year of the church's foundation, 1692. It was extraordinarily popular in the 1970s but has more recently largely returned to the obscurity from which it came. It offers a number of platitudes, among them "Be yourself" and "Be gentle with yourself"; but it also has some deeper wisdom, such as the observation "Many fears are born of fatigue and loneliness."

If this book speaks in an assertive, direct voice, it does so in the spirit of the prose poem that inspired it. I hope that readers who are not used to receiving such unabashed counsel will quickly recognize that I am invariably addressing myself. Much more than to Ehrmann, the style and content of my words are indebted to Thomas Traherne. His *Centuries of Meditations* have had the effect on me that I hope this volume will have on its readers. Traherne is always teasing, dancing, inciting, and pirouetting. But he has the ability to stay still, and dwell deeply on just one moment, one artifact, one insight—as Mother Julian once cradled a hazelnut, and as God treasures us. It is such intensity, such wonder, such concentration, such joy that this book seeks to enliven. It is an invitation to a way of being, a way of becoming fully alive, in which reading, contemplating, celebrating, discovering, and praying meet, and gradually become indistinguishable from one another.

What I want is for a person to ask, "How should I feel when I have prayed?"—and for their companion to reply, "You know how you felt when you finished reading *Walk Humbly*? It should feel like that."

1

Be Humble

Be humble. Ponder your moment—your location in time. There are things that abide forever; and there are things that last for a limited period. The things that abide forever we call *essence*; the things that last for a limited period we call *existence*.

We human beings are in the second category. We exist: we think that because we exist—because we are aware that we exist—we are the heart, the center, the purpose of all things. But we tend to forget that existence isn't all there is. We are missing something: something important, something vital. Existence is not the same as essence. Existence is subject to change and decay—and death. Essence isn't. Yes, we do indeed exist, and that is precious, and remarkable, and the basis of all the joys of life. But we are not essences: we are not eternal, ineradicable, permanent. We are not essential. We are simply existential. There is, without us. Take us away and there still is. We are contingent—our being depends on the existence of others. We crave independence, but it is an illusion, a fantasy: we never could be, never shall be, independent, and there would be no joy in being so. The longing for independence is the aspiration to be an essence: the secret of happiness is to learn instead to exist.

Once we relax, and cease trying to be an essence—*the* essence—and only then, can we begin to enjoy the fact that we exist. It's said there are three answers to every question: "yes," "no," and "it depends"—and the answer is nearly always "it depends," because you can arrive at the clarity and simplicity of "yes" or "no" only by excluding all additional information. But that additional information is what makes up the stuff of life— relationship, context, history, possibility, likelihood, surprise, accident. To exist is to depend—to be contingent—to be part of that additional information. We're never in the clear. We're always subject to unforeseen circumstances, liable to unexpected alterations, inclined to unpredictable outcomes. The question is not, "How can we not depend?" The real question is, "How can we depend on the right things?" In existence, there's no such thing as certainty. The opposite of chance isn't certainty: it's trust. Life isn't about excluding chance and establishing certainty: it's about identifying what, whom, and how to trust.

Why are we here? Not because we chose to be. How did our existence come about? Not because it was essential. We exist—everything exists—because the essence of things, of all things, in the depths of its mysteries, brought into being something that was not essential, something that was not like itself, but something . . . else. It need not have been so. There is no inevitable explanation why it was, and is, so. But so it is. We are part of that "else." We are not the original "something." We don't know if we're the center of that "else," or the purpose of that "else," but on the scientific and historical evidence, it seems unlikely. We don't know whether that "else" might be viable or even better off without us, but it seems more than probable. So we're not just inessential to essence— we're not even existential to existence. Existing is not about establishing and conforming to what must be so—it's about enjoying the precarious discovery that nothing must be so.

Existence very capably regenerates and reproduces itself. But existence as a *whole* cannot generate itself. If there is indeed existence, of which we are a part, though not an inevitable part (and there must be existence, otherwise how could this interaction of writing and reading be taking place?), then there must be essence—unchanging, without decay, not subject to death—above and beyond that existence, bringing it about, sustaining it, replenishing it, and abiding after it is gone. But we have no direct, unmistakable, and incontrovertible access from our realm of existence to that sphere of essence. Which is why identifying the nature of that essence (and even asserting the very foundational quality of that essence) will always be controversial and disputed; and which is also why there will always be a temptation to elevate some or all characteristics of existence to the level of essence. Sometimes we get exasperated and seek at least some firm ground given that essence is so impenetrable. Sometimes we proudly assume that the highest glories of existence need not (or could not) be surpassed. But this is to deny the character of existence: for it is part of the nature of existence never to be able to be certain about essence.

There could have been no existence. There could have been nothing. Perhaps there was, for an almost infinite period—a period that can't be measured in time, because time is a characteristic of existence. To say there could have been—may even yet be—nothing is not to deny that there is an essence. We assume there must be an essence because something must have brought about and must sustain and replenish and will surely abide beyond existence. But there could have been nothing beyond essence. That, in fact, would seem more likely. This is where humility begins: with the recognition that it would have been simpler, more plausible, less troublesome, tidier for there to have been no existence; in practice, nothing. Yet despite that more sanguine eventuality, here we are. A twinkle in the imagination of essence maybe, but existing nonetheless. Humility is founded on the realization that it would have been much more probable that we would not have existed: and it is only some balance between chance and love that has made it otherwise. Establishing the degree of that balance between chance and love is the process of discovering truth.

To begin to wonder is to settle on what it could possibly have been that induced essence to conceive, trigger, initiate, or imagine existence. Wonder is the capacity to appreciate that it might not have been so, that it might yet have been very different, that it might not be so for much longer or ever again—but it still, nonetheless, is. Awe is the inclination to perceive the depth, texture, dimensions, and extent of the attention, care, wisdom, and delight—yet also the grief, loss, longing, and disappointment—that underpin the inception of existence, the transition from eternity to time, from boundlessness to circumscription, from the elusive and immortal to the tangible and fragile. Gratitude is apprehension that this balance of chance and love has brought about every ingredient of the circumstances that brought me into existence, that there is nothing whatsoever for which I can claim the credit, that it is all entirely gift, that I shall never be able to discharge my consequent debt, and that I must therefore remain suspended in dumbfounded astonishment and delirious reverence. Humility is that hallowed clearing in the forest of existence where wonder, awe, and gratitude meet, dance, play, and exult.

For essence to issue in existence requires a constellation of instigation and withdrawal, of sustained intention that yet refrains from control, of meticulous direction and yet relaxed permission. Most of all, it requires risk—risk that things may unravel, sour, hurt, distort, and need sacrificial attention and utter devotion to be drawn back toward glory. Ponder this: what is the name we give to this constellation, to this foundational yet reckless risk without which there is nothing? The name we give is love. Love isn't the afterthought, a sentimental alternative to the harshness of time and chance, conflict and death; love is the beginning, the cause, the formula for what makes essence issue in existence, the imagination that translates "maybe" into "be." Love is the pivot around which the circle of life rotates. Love is not simply a gallant protest against the ravages of loss, poison, decay, violence, isolation; it is the assertion, reassertion, primal surfacing of the original cause and ultimate purpose of existence.

Love and chance aren't opposites. It's not that existence is caused by either random explosion or purposive creation; the process by which essence issues in existence, the constellation of determining yet allowing, directing yet involving—the process of love—is one in which chance is incorporated into reason. Love is not about control; it is precisely the willingness, the urge, the resolve to wait in attentive patience with that other that tantalizingly fails to fulfill desires and expectations or excruciatingly intends to subvert kindness and benevolence. The creativity and improvisation of the coming-into-being of existence thus assumes chance within the panoply of love. Evolution tells us that existence is perpetuated through the impulse to survive and the haphazard pattern of mutation; but love is always a constant process of improvisation to incorporate and of adaptation to accommodate the unexpected, uncharacteristic, and sometimes unwelcome. Sooner or later any kind of love faces the fact that it must renounce control.

More profitable than to sift the ocean of chance for sparkling glints of love is to contemplate the myriad moments when the chain of being could have snapped such that your life would never have been. In perhaps every generation a life could have gone a different direction, been prematurely foreshortened perhaps; the two lives from which each of your ancestors were conceived might never have crossed paths, been drawn together, been fertile in conceiving those whose birth eventually led to the moment you began. Reaching back to the mists of origin, before humans took shape, the stepladder of your prehistory might at any moment have come loose and in so doing snatched away the possibility of your existence. And so for us all. Reflect on how many of your ancestors clung to life to the point where they could conceive the one whose birth eventually led to yours. Realize by how fragile a thread their existence hung, and behold how the miracle of your birth is made up of a concatenation of other such miracles. Your existence is a thing most wonderful: almost too wonderful to be.

Your parents crystallize the marvel of your existence. You did not choose to exist; you did not even consent. You did not select your parents; you cannot begin to imagine the infinitesimal improbability of their union, and of that union conceiving you. You may discern their uniqueness; you are doubtless familiar with their ordinariness. You are perhaps best placed to perceive their fallibility. You may owe as much to their nourishing and saving you in your upbringing as you do to the careful or clumsy way they engendered you. Regardless of their perfections or fragilities, simply accept that you would not exist without them. They may be to blame for much; but without them you would not be alive to apportion such blame. To honor your parents is to recall daily that your existence was not of your making and its purpose is never simply of your determining.

Be humble. Because you depend. You depend on whatever it was that made essence issue in existence. You are part of that "else" that means there is more than simply something. You are part of that existence that is less plausible than there simply being nothing—that has no necessity. You hang by a fragile thread that traces back through countless generations, each one of which is, in its way, precarious and unlikely and remarkable and miraculous. You remain in unquenchable debt to a balance of love and chance that are not opposites but deeply involve each other. Each of these contingencies is focused in the mystery, mundanity, and miracle of your parents. And to nav-

igate this life you need not the knowledge of necessity, the conviction of certainty, or the assumption of
entitlement, but the establishment, cultivation, and
restoration of trust.

2

Be Grateful

Be grateful. From 1921, Mahatma Gandhi made a habit of appearing in public dressed in a simple dhoti and shawl. A dhoti is a long rectangular stretch of cloth, wrapped around the hips, then draped through the legs, and finally knotted at the waist. It is the clothing of the common people. Gandhi adopted this form of clothing to represent his solidarity with the masses in their struggle for freedom and security. The apparent simplicity of Gandhi's appearance contrasted with the sophistication of his tactics and his campaign. The last Viceroy of India, Earl Mountbatten of Burma, observed ruefully, "You have no idea how many people it takes to keep that man in poverty."

What Mountbatten witnessed about Gandhi, a careful spectator could infer about any of us. It requires a company of angels to keep any single one of us in the life to which we are accustomed. We are each like a tightrope walker who thinks she's balancing by sheer skill, only to find a forest of hands supporting each end of her horizontal pole and some gentle shoulders keeping her ankles steady.

As we lie in bed, the cotton in our sheets has been picked by low-paid labor; the mattress beneath us has been constructed in a factory whose conditions we seldom imagine. When we rise to take a wash, we use shampoo and soap and toothpaste from countries and conditions and cultures and climates we might shrink from if we ever troubled to discover what they were. We pour a bowl of cereal whose contents have been through many hands before they reached our kitchen, and we find a teabag whose leaves have been garnered by a person stooping for many hours in baking sun for little reward. We finger a phone or switch on a radio, the technical elements of which have been extracted from a mine whose resources dominate the economy and the politics of a country quite possibly overshadowed and pressurized in numerous ways by our own. We head to work or college or school in a car or bus or train, burning fuel laid down over millions of years that can't be replenished, that is extracted in demanding ways, and whose consumption in large quantities jeopardizes the well-being and even survival of people, wildlife, and the ecosphere across the world and into the indefinite future.

When and if we do work, we find ourselves part of a network of suppliers and customers, equally dependent on both, and subject to the fashions of taste or interest, the swings of the weather or the economy, and the trends of political or social ideology. More tangibly, we find ourselves paralyzed and exasperated if our boss, our colleague, or the person reporting to us is idle, inefficient, selfish, neglectful, incompetent, or disrespectful. We can do almost anything, however challenging, if we can form a good team with those around us; almost nothing, however elementary, if we can't. When we leave a job it's the people, not the projects, we remember; if we find joy, it's because we did something together, with each person playing their part, deepening esteem for respective personalities and roles as we recognize it takes a village to raise a child, or a barn, or a standard.

There are plenty of parts of life we don't want to see. If we eat an egg, we may prefer to ignore the conditions in which the chicken has been confined. If we enjoy a beef steak or veal cutlet or leg of lamb, we may close our eyes to the nature of an animal's life, the conditions of its transport, the nature of an abattoir. We may be careful how we divide up our organic, recyclable, and general waste, but we may not ever behold the realities of how trash is disposed of; the kinds of work involved; the smells, dirt, and discomforts of doing so. We seldom ask whose sweat produced our shoes, our computer, our shirt (which we boast of having bought so cheaply); and we scarcely pause to consider, when we get a bargain, which link in the supply chain got no reward this time.

We sense our vulnerability when we feel our health falter. Then we enter a spider's web of medical professionals in which we are a tiny insect. But just imagine trying to be our own physiotherapist, let alone our own dentist or optician; we are at the mercy of such skills and assistance. For most, much the same is true when a house requires a builder or a car awaits a mechanic or a bathroom needs a plumber or a computer requires a technician. Only a small minority don't find themselves dependent on family, friends, or the state when they fall on hard times—face unemployment, struggle to pay bills, go through a family break-up, have a spouse in prison, or lose their home to floods or fire. And there are few, at least in the developed world, who would prepare the dead body of their loved one for its last farewell—let alone bury or cremate it themselves.

The commodification of entertainment inclines us to look to those in the public eye to offer us distraction, diversion, delight, and delectation. There's a big sporting event on tonight—why can't there also be one tomorrow? What does it matter if the players are tired? I want my favorite player on the team—so what if he's injured? He should take a painkiller—who cares if the side effects trouble him in his later years? I like that series of novels—why can't the author publish sequels more frequently? I'm dying to see the next film about that detective, I'm curious to know more of the personal life of that newsreader, I'm always up for salacious information about the politicians of that party.... Not only do I depend on others for my food, clothing, shelter, and employment, but in my leisure time I join the voracious consumption of human performance and appearance that keeps me amused and intrigued.

The vortex of contemporary society is to zero all these forms of complex dependence down to two levers: the mobile phone and the credit card; the one to manage interactions, the other to cover costs. Both are forms of reduction—ways to simplify, streamline, accelerate, or eradicate relationship. But the result of so doing is to hide the reality of dependence, and thus turn relationship into an abstraction—even, perhaps, an imposition. And this erodes our awareness of our limitation and mortality into a fantasy of unencumbered reward. What gets lost is gratitude.

Gratitude is the moment we turn from seeing dependence as a burden and begin to see it as a gift. Gratitude is the window we are given into how dependence creates relationship. A person might say, "If it weren't for my poor eyesight, I wouldn't need to ask a neighbor child's help reading my mail and opening tins of dogfood. If I didn't have a child in my house helping me open tins, I wouldn't be able to feed my dog regularly. If I didn't have a dog, I wouldn't have heard the noise and disturbance when my fridge malfunctioned and began to smoke. Because of the dog's barking I was able to press the panic button in my home and support quickly arrived and my kitchen was saved and my belongings were rescued; perhaps I and even my neighbors would otherwise have lost our lives. A whole chain of events tracing back to my poor eyesight and the way it created the need for relationship."

A person who lived close by might say, "Because my near neighbor had poor eyesight I used to go round to her house during the week to open her emails and letters and read them to her. And because I loved her dog I used to go round more often than she needed me to. And because I got used to talking to her about her messages and entering into her personal world, I felt more comfortable sharing with her my difficulty in sleeping, my nightmares, my trembling hands, my confused and patchy memories of my real father whom we don't see anymore. And that was how I got so interested in care of the elderly, because in her I saw both a gentle soul who was able to hear my distress, and also a person whose vulnerability made her subject to the kind of harm I now realize I suffered as a young child. And I came to pioneer a new form of care for seniors, which made me famous in my field. And all because I had a near neighbor and I loved her dog."

Thus does dependence create relationship, and relationship unearth untold gifts and assets and blessings and innovation. And gratitude names the process by which the deficits of poor eyesight and creeping infirmity and distressing childhood experience and troubling nocturnal despair turn, through our becoming open to one another's gentle companionship and unexpected grace, into the assets of vocational discovery, career advancement, medico-social advance, and saved lives. So much of current cultural development tries to address the challenges and traumas of these two neighbors through solutions that can be bought with a card or accessed through a phone. But gratitude knows what such solutions can never comprehend. What gratitude knows is that existence is made up of setbacks, mistakes, challenges, and obstacles, and it is in facing and tackling and sometimes enduring those adversities that mortality is discovered, dependence recognized, and relationship sought. And it is in such relationship, and the unanticipated benefits that accompany it, that true joy lies.

The term we give to utter dependence—dependence that is entirely deficit, dependence that has no access to its own resources, no opportunity to reflect on just social structures, no resort to skills or income to withstand crisis, no seductive diversion to distract from distressing thoughts—is the deathbed. On the deathbed we have a choice. We can fervidly seek an escape, searching through the labyrinth for an exit, relentlessly hoping that a secret path will appear, a route to independence will be disclosed, life's lessons may be deferred till another dawn, and reality will be kept at bay. Or we can yield, stop resisting, and finally acknowledge that independence was a chimera, based on false overestimation of our own faculties and fortune, and false underestimation of what the world and our neighbors contribute to our well-being. There is no limit to what can be achieved so long as you don't mind who gets the credit. The deathbed is the name for the moment when we stop trying to re-narrate the story of our lives as ones in which we accumulate so much talent, accomplishment, charm, skill, wit, and luck that we ultimately dodge mortality and get out of life alive.

On the deathbed we discover that all the things we thought were ours—our achievements, rights, possessions, entitlements, fallbacks, supports—

were never really ours after all. Our breath was not ours, but was made up of air we didn't make that came from outside us, and was breathed by lungs we didn't construct, enfleshed by food we didn't direct, processed by a stomach we couldn't control. Our consciousness was not ours, but was our awareness of our existence—whose beginnings we didn't prompt and whose joint continuation we could never make permanent. Our body was not ours; we didn't form it in our mother's womb, we didn't birth it, we didn't create its DNA, we cannot reproduce its identical replica, we cannot withstand its inescapable demise, we cannot preserve one tiny atom of it to take with us wherever we're headed.

Likewise in a thousand ways our life has been preserved while we have scarcely noticed, have hardly paused to acknowledge. The parent who fed us when we didn't know how to get food for ourselves. The teacher who plucked us out when we fell headlong into the deep end of the pool. The friend who pulled us back when we stepped out in front of traffic that was coming from an unanticipated direction. The sibling who told us not to eat that attractive-looking root. The companion who held our hand when the rock gave way beneath our feet on a mountain hike. The passenger who shouted when we were headed at top speed through a red signal. Gratitude names the way we finally realize the story could have been so different, so much shorter, so much more painful. And others, not ourselves, made it not so. And for others, tragically, it was so. And is so.

Thus the deathbed is where life begins. Not life as existence, or extent; but life as gift, as gratitude, as grace: as a walk of humility. The words "Thank you" say, it could have been so terrible, impoverished, flat, without you; but they also say, I have become determined and practiced at seeing the glory in the darkness as well as the light. Even setbacks have taught me wisdom and mercy. I have become defined not by bitterness, but by discovery and by compassion. If I have learned to be grateful, I have resolved to be what only I can be, but to want what everyone else can have as well.

3

Be Your Own Size

Be your own size. There are 300 billion stars in our own galaxy and 100 billion galaxies in the universe. The diameter of the observable universe is around 90 billion light-years: what lies beyond that is unknown. As for Earth, it's not even at the center of our solar system; the solar system is by no means the center of the Milky Way; and the Milky Way is nowhere near the center of the universe. Those looking for the significance of Earth, of life, of humankind, let alone their own life, are not going to find it in relation to the universe; they need to look elsewhere. The universe, understood as time and space, is a lesson in utter, yet not infinite, humility.

Our insecurity impels us to say, "Don't start the party until I arrive!" The other characters in the drama may have an identity independent of us and a validity not devoted to inflating our importance, but we are nonetheless bent on fostering a party so intense and absorbing that it obscures the reality of everything outside it, for as long as possible—thus creating the illusion of permanence. Life is in many senses a party—an organized attempt to draw people, circumstances, and experience within a confined space for a limited time so as to condense existence and make it effervescent, fruitful, and abundant—as if in defiance of the cold, mundane, unforgiving actuality outside.

But this is to found existence on a falsehood—to make life an escape into fantasy. Instead, truth can only begin with taking in the enormity of that banquet of which you are the very tiniest ingredient. To pretend you are in the center, to imagine you are the link in the chain that connects all the others, to suppose that the theater is so small that everyone can see you, to occupy yourself so fervidly that you forget the extent of the universe beyond—all these are understandable reactions amid the panic of infinitesimal presence and utter insignificance; but they are all constructed falsehoods. They are houses built on sand.

We take for granted, when the Sun sets, that it will rise again next day. If it wasn't so, what could we do about it? We may say, "It must be so"—we may point to the gravity that makes the Earth circle the Sun or the seasons that have passed one after another since the dawn of world and time, or the logic that says that light is about the almost inexhaustible inferno of the Sun and not about the fragile ecology of the Earth. But our incapacity to affect whether the Sun rises reflects our smallness in the face of the most significant determinants of our existence.

So intolerable is the recognition of this incapacity that we create a party—a party that includes only certain people, concerns only particular things, values only that which we can comprehend, lasts only a limited time, seeks only that which we can control, encompasses only that which has human dimensions. The party is about the struggle for power, the quest for security, the striving for belonging, the defining of identity, the need to survive, the longing to create, the hunger to possess. Such passions and preoccupations are so consuming they absorb almost all humankind's attention, energy, and awareness.

Finding meaning has to begin by stepping outside that party—to go out on the balcony and behold the stars. And what do the stars tell us? One must let go of the illusion of permanence: what one does for good may indeed be good, but that good can't be measured by how lasting it is. What one does for ill may indeed be ill, but mercifully that ill may last even less time than the good. Consider the much-lauded aspiration of "making a difference." While often a worthy encouragement to seek the common good, it is, in the light of the breadth and longevity of the universe, a sentiment of either hubris or narcissism. Where does wisdom lie? In the slow realization that actions and interventions are to be evaluated not by the impact they make (since results are invariably unpredictable and inevitably transitory) but by their intrinsic quality and by whether they bear the hallmark of a better spirit, or herald the advent of a truer society.

Percy Shelley wrote of "a traveller from an antique land" who described the sight of two "vast and trunkless legs of stone" standing in the desert, not far from "a shattered visage" with its "frown, and wrinkled lip, and sneer of cold command." The pedestal of that visage announces, "My name is Ozymandias, King of

Kings; look on my Works, ye Mighty, and despair!"
Powerful and intimidating these words may once
have been, but today "nothing beside remains"; on
the contrary, stretching in all directions from what is
now no more than a "colossal Wreck" there is nothing
but unmerciful desert: "boundless and bare the lone
and level sands stretch far away." This is more than
an ironic reflection on how the mighty are fallen. It's
a statement about our place in the universe, a recognition that, as Macbeth realized, life is a walking
shadow, in which we strut and fret our hour upon
the stage, generating sound and fury without abiding significance. Shelley's lone and level sands could
as well be the boundless and bare stretches of empty
space as galaxy unfolds into galaxy.

Before we say to someone, "Do you know who I
am?" it's as well to ask ourselves, in light of the scale
of the universe and its venerable age, "Who exactly
am I?"[1] "Who I am" may mean my genealogy, or my
social location and sense of entitlement; it may mean
who my people are, where I feel I belong, where I
came from—in short, whose I am; or it could mean
what role I perform, what title I bear, how famous,
honored, powerful, accomplished I am, in ways I

have come to assume everyone I meet should already know. But such designations are like Ozymandias's shattered visage and trunkless legs in the boundless dunes: they are doomed attempts to spit against the wind, to prevent the tide of eternity engulfing the precious sandcastle of a human life. Anyone who asks, "Do you know who I am?" needs to be prepared to hear the answer, "No—do you?" Responding to that answer requires us to wear our own size, to locate ourselves in eternal time and almost infinite space, and to regard any respect we might receive as a gift and any honor we might accrue as sheer grace.

This is not just about realizing we are tiny beings and our existence scarcely scratches the surface of the universe. It's also about agency. If we look simply to the Earth, which we share with so many living beings, many of the tiny ones scurry and multiply and in hidden ways make it possible for you to breathe, to heal, to digest, to sleep. The whole ecology of the planet attains an equilibrium that human beings as often inhibit as advance, but still is of breathtaking interlocking complexity. As is well known, wolves were reintroduced to Yellowstone National Park after a seventy-year absence.[2] Their presence changed the behavior of the deer that hitherto had grazed away most of the low-lying vegetation. Quickly plants and trees sprang up: birds inhabited them and beavers emerged to feed off the bark. The beavers made dams, which attracted fish and other river life. Meanwhile the wolves hunted the coyotes, creating opportunities for mice and rabbits, and invigorating their predators—hawks, weasels, foxes, badgers. Bears, eagles, and ravens also benefited from the carcasses the wolves left behind. Moreover, the stable vegetation strengthened the banks of the rivers and enabled more wildlife to settle there. Thus the wolves even changed the physical geography of the region, noted for its geysers and the magnificent Grand Canyon of the Yellowstone River. Such a story, known as a trophic cascade, demonstrates not only the wonder of Earth's interrelationships but also the way humankind is neither the orchestrator nor the monarch of those connections.

And it is not just the larger mammals and plants. Humankind depends on so many tiny creatures. Ants are crucial for decomposition, aerating soil, recycling nutrients, and transporting seeds. Termites are vital for breaking down cellulose and thus recycling fallen leaves. Bats consume pest insects and pollinate plants, and their guano disperses seeds. Birds do almost all of the things ants, termites, and bats do, while bees pollinate more than all of the above put together. Human beings are junior members of a team to which most of us don't even realize we belong. We're not just at the end of a human supply chain or an animal food chain but in a web of an ecosystem of plants, insects, and creatures of every size and dimension.

Within the human body we depend on a host of microorganisms we seldom acknowledge and are inclined to regard as unclean. There are bacteria that release acids to ward off other virulent bacteria, that break down plant molecules that humans cannot digest on their own, that help infants digest milk, and that allow blood-clotting mechanisms to function properly. Our lives rest in an ecology we will never live long enough to comprehend, still less thank.

The amazing thing is not that we suffer, or struggle, or die; it is that we exist at all. We are surrounded by a magnificent and almost infinitely extended orchestra, but we insist on playing our lone instrument. However clumsily and tunelessly we play it, however much logic tells us we can't hope to be playing it for long, however inclined we are for short or protracted periods to play it with another or a handful of others, we carelessly or studiously disregard the orchestra of microorganisms, tiny creatures, larger mammals, vegetation and minerals, weather and seasons, solar system, galaxy, and universe that extends far beyond our comprehension and imagination. In so doing we forget who we are, how much we matter, and what size we are.

4

Be Gentle

Be gentle. The ninefold fruit of the Spirit is love, joy, peace, patience, kindness, goodness, faithfulness, gentleness, self-control (Galatians 5:22). What is self-control? It cannot simply be the suppression of all desire to have, consume, possess, or see. Rather, it is the appropriate allocation of desire over a longer timescale. If you seek the honorable things, the things of lasting value, that never run out—or, as Matthew tells us Jesus put it, if you seek first the kingdom of God (Matthew 6:33)—then in due time, all other things will be added to you as well. Which means you seek those things with gentleness. They are easily dropped, broken, squashed, or suffocated, and must therefore be cherished, treasured, honored, and cultivated. Self-control is the ability to cherish what others might grab, to treasure what one might be tempted to snatch. In other words, to be gentle.

But is that not equally true of patience? Patience grows from the perception of what lies ahead, and the hope and trust that this future, whether attained by endeavor or received as a gift, will fulfill the lack that would otherwise flood the consciousness. If this satisfaction will undoubtedly be attained, there's no need to ruin the present simply because it doesn't yet resemble the future. Instead, one can enjoy the character of the present and not require it to conform to the shape of things to come. But if they are coming, they are already for the most part yours; and the time between their anticipated achievement and their final fulfillment can be doubly blessed—blessed by expectation, and blessed meanwhile by other perceptions that would have been obscured had the longed-for thing been already here. And that double blessing is what evokes gentleness. Such gentleness is made up of relish in the things that have not been sought but nonetheless line the route, yet at the same time deeper respect and understanding for the things that have been pursued, in recognition that they can't be taken for granted like things that appear instantly, on demand.

Imagine a couple who yearn to conceive a child. Their expectation may turn to desperation, their confidence to entitlement, their planning to demanding. In consequence their whole world may become impoverished: their lovemaking may become not tender but utilitarian, their friendships with their peers may be colored by grief or poisoned by envy, their daily work may become passionless and burdensome, their domestic existence may be empty and eroded. In short, gentleness may gradually evaporate. But a couple who find the grace to wait with patience may discover a new level of gentleness. They may volunteer at a center for families in crisis, recognizing that not all experiences of raising children are joyous or straightforward; they may support victims of domestic abuse, perhaps becoming more grateful for the gestures of understanding that keep their own relationship free from exasperation, manipulation, or violence; they may walk with mothers who have given a child up for adoption or women who have had a termination, and thus perceive many twists in the kaleidoscope of parental circumstance. Whether they finally conceive, bear, and raise children or not, their patience may yield a gentleness more precious than any desired outcome. Gentleness means creating time and space to explore who and where you are, rather than lapse into remorse, resentment, or regret about who or where you're not, and growing in the grace to let others do the same.

This is also true of kindness. We take for granted that we act with honor, dignity, respect, and thoughtfulness toward our kin—although it is not always so. But to extend such actions toward simple acquaintances, even strangers, is to expand the range of one's kin so as to create a people, a nation—a world. Kindness is treating those outside the circle as if they were in the circle, offering to a person who would otherwise be isolated a gesture of kinship, noticing another's mild disadvantage or major setback and making such a moment an opportunity for the establishment of relationship, creation of tenderness, dismantlement of distance, overcoming of alienation. To be kind requires empathy, a sustained or fleeting perception of what it's like to be another person, how that person may be in discomfort or jeopardy, and how one's own simple engagement, support, or praise may materially, emotionally, or vitally ameliorate their circumstances or defray their distress. To be kind to yourself means to recognize that you often, perhaps invariably, treat others with an understanding and tenderness that you customarily withhold from yourself, and to resolve to regard yourself as the first among the others you are called to honor. This is gentleness: the moment when you apprehend that self-care and social relations can be built out of habits of daily understanding and empathy, in which you assume the other is in need of encouragement, appreciation, and recognition unless proved otherwise, and is at heart at least as fragile as you know yourself to be.

Thus gentleness is a salad derived from kindness, patience, and self-control. But the gentleness that arises from humility recognizes the clumsiness of our tendency to brush into or tread upon the vulnerability, innocence, or grief of others, perhaps most especially when we're convinced our course of action is noble. Remember the physician's mantra, "First, do no harm." Our actions hover between hubris and diffidence, arrogance and laziness, ignorance and pusillanimity. There is very seldom a straight choice between doing something (presumably to save, rescue, transform, or redeem) and doing nothing. There is almost always the possibility of working alongside the person in danger so both you and they contribute appropriate skills and insights to address their peril; and there is invariably the option of remaining in solidarity with the distressed person while they resolve their situation in ways you could have had no comprehension of and with an outcome incalculably more sustainable and beneficial to them. It is very seldom the case that a crisis is so configured that all the jeopardy (and nothing else) lies with the person in the predicament, while all the resources, intelligence, wisdom, experience, and power (and no mixed motive) lie with oneself. And even when it does seem so configured, or largely so, there is no guarantee that our own intervention will alter things for the better.

Gentleness does not mean walking by on the other side as a matter of policy. But it does mean assuming that our first gift is presence and attention, in other words human engagement and sustained empathy. Such involvement may develop, if appropriate and invited, into participation and partnership, that is to say, a willingness to struggle alongside the person in trouble, using or not using our own honed or previously unexploited skills, over the short or long haul. It may require alerting or referring to a third party better able—or better placed, resourced, or qualified—to assist. Only if a process of discernment judges all these options to be exhausted or inapplicable does singlehanded "rescue" enter the frame; and humility demands that a due assessment be made of whether such rescue may fail, have no positive effect, or in fact make things worse.

Such caution is illuminated by the words of William Blake: "We are put on earth a little space, That we may learn to bear the beams of love." There's so much that we've never even paused to imagine. When we look to right and left, we see others who know about as little as we do. We scarcely know the conscious motivations, external factors, or internal drives that trigger friends or strangers to act as they do; we hardly know our own motives! We research and attend to the causes of meteoric events or earthly tremors, animal behavior or population swings; but in the end so much is mystery, and most is unexplained. We can be ignited to rage when we see a young man hurtle into an elderly woman on a street, little knowing he is seeking to divert her path from a piece of falling scaffolding. We can be quick to condemn a woman creating an unfortunate scene in the auditorium at a theatrical performance, unaware that she is experiencing her first-ever epileptic fit. We can be horrified that a car veers off the road, assuming the driver is drunk or reckless, only later to discover she has had a heart attack. We can be disgusted that an ungrateful student falls asleep during a carefully prepared presentation by an earnest peer; our condemnation may be out of our mouth before we understand he's been struggling with narcolepsy and cannot control the onset of excessive drowsiness.

In Plato's *Apology*, Socrates judges that he himself has no knowledge, and asks politicians, poets, and craftspeople if they have greater knowledge than he. Politicians claim wisdom but lack knowledge; poets have the ability to move people, but they know not the meaning of their words; craftspeople indeed have knowledge, but only within their own narrow field. Socrates concludes that he is wiser than others in that he doesn't claim to know things he in fact does not know. Hence the nowhere-recorded but nonetheless widely quoted expression attributed to him, "I am wise because I know that I know nothing." If this is true for the workings of the world and the universe, how much more true is it for the movements of the human heart and soul: the heart has its reasons the reason knows not of, as Blaise Pascal noted. Fathoming reason is a perpetual project: plumbing the heart is an impossible one. Fools rush in where angels fear to tread. Our clumsiness knows no bounds: we can trespass on a tender disclosure, a first artistic foray, an intimate fear of shame, a brave attempt to face criticism with dignity, a wounded fledgling confidence, a long-forestalled moment of candor. As W. B. Yeats enjoined, "Tread softly because you tread on my dreams."

Have you never rolled your eyes in exasperation at a driver who would not yield to you, only sometime later to be so fixated on getting urgently to your destination that you chose today to be first at every light and regard all other road users as obstacles to your plans? Have you never despised a shiftless, good-for-nothing beggar near a rail station, only to find yourself later, on a dark and unforgiving night, stripped of your wallet, phone, and keys and depending on the mercy of strangers to get you home and safe? Have you never judged a ragged parent with a screaming child and wondered why they had to visit the grocery store at such a conflictual moment, only to be in charge of an even more challenging infant, at a still less appropriate juncture, perhaps in the very same store another day? Have you never berated the voters of another political party for their dim-witted attitudes and uninformed opinions, only to change circumstances and move across country and take up with a different crowd of people and find yourself espousing judgments that years ago you'd have derided? Have you never been offended that two lovers couldn't wait to express their feelings, wished that they could have shown more respect for those around them, wondered why they had no fear that the memories of these unguarded moments would later come to humiliate them, only years later, surprised by joy, to find yourself imitating the exact same people upon whom you once looked down?

How often have you looked upon what another person said or did with horror, fury, or scorn, only to find yourself, ten years (or ten minutes) later, saying or doing much the same? Be sparing with your horror, fury, and scorn, lest they rebound on you and make you lamentable in your own sight. People tend to do the best they can with what they have and what they know. A little generosity of heart inclines us to look to our fellow creatures with gentleness rather than bitterness, compassion rather than anger, understanding rather than condemnation. As Maya Angelou put it, "Do the best you can until you know better. Then when you know better, do better."

5

Be a Person of Praise

Be a person of praise. Humility and gratitude are the fertile ground for the cherishing of a story. There will always be stories that demand to take precedence over other stories. Perhaps a family story, as if one tribe— or race—could somehow embody all truth, all purpose, all meaning. Maybe a national story, pretending that within certain borders, or on a particular island, or among those who speak a specific language there is a residual character, distinctive identity, or manifest destiny. Such assertions are untrue, although it seems sometimes to take terrible war or appalling suffering to expose the lie they promote.

One familiar story has no such vainglory. It's told not for anyone's aggrandizement, but for the praise of its author and the blessings bestowed on those for whom it has come to pass. It offers three reasons to consider the other side of humility and to wear our own size.

The first is that we human beings are the form essence chose to take when it entered existence. This is the astonishing claim of this story. On one starry night, displaced by migration, in a hostile political climate, surrounded by animals, from an unwed mother living homeless in a strange town, essence entered existence. Essence, which we could call by a hundred names but we most often call God; essence, which could have remained alone without ever conceiving of existence; essence, which would most straightforwardly have left things as nothing but out of utmost grace initiated existence—that essence made itself part of existence. The Word became flesh.

That's what's unique about this story and the culture that it fosters. There's nothing special about recognizing the difference between essence and existence. Most accounts of reality do, because it's hard not to accept a distinction between what lasts forever and what lasts for just a period of time. Likewise, there's nothing special about having a code of ethics. Almost every culture has its ethical code, although there are obviously significant differences between them. There's nothing special about having particular buildings or rituals or even having a holy book. There are equivalents in many, perhaps most cultures. No, this is the heart of this story: the essence of all things became part of existence—subject to change, decay, and death, just like us.

It wasn't necessary. It wasn't any more necessary than essence creating existence in the first place. But once you grasp it, you can see that the two events are as linked as a pair of shoes. Why did essence create existence? No one could possibly know, until this very moment, when essence becomes part of existence. Here we discover the answer to perhaps the biggest question of all: why is there something rather than nothing? The answer is, because essence—or God, as we usually say—always intended to be our companion, to be with us. That's what the word "Jesus" represents: God's eternal purpose to be with us, which triggered the whole mystery of existence from beginning to end. Jesus isn't an afterthought that came into existence when essence realized existence was going awry: Jesus is the whole meaning and purpose for existence in the first place. Jesus is the reason we exist.

Behold how this reverses the usual way of asking the question of why we exist. When we place ourselves at the center of all things, we make existence primary, and we demand proofs of God's existence through our getting a job or an end to war or our recovery from a painful illness. But existence isn't primary. That's what essence is. Trying to reach God from existence is as absurd and impossible as throwing a stone and trying to hit a cloud. However noble our endeavors, they are simply locked within existence. However sublime our glimpse of beauty, it is no more than a passing shadow. However bold our grasp of truth, it is a bridge attached on the side of existence that yet lacks any mooring on the side of essence. We discover God for one reason alone: because God reaches us. Essence becomes existence. Jesus becomes human. The Word becomes flesh.

The second moment of grace is that essence imbues existence with elements of wonder through which existence may find traction on the path of grace, like a car whose wheels are fitted with chains to help it drive through snow. Just as creation endows creatures with the means of their own survival and the capacity to learn to thrive, so the Holy Spirit clothes the church with the garments of salvation. Through these means, essence draws existence to itself as a magnet draws iron. Among these means is scripture. In reading, performing, and returning to scripture, the church becomes inscribed in the story, discovers the author's house style, and learns to recognize the ways of God beyond the penumbra of its own influence. Then there are the sacraments. In baptism the church is conformed to the body of Christ, and disciples share the experience of dying to self and living to God. In the Eucharist the church enacts God's new society in which forgiven disciples bring forward fruit of the earth and human hands, transformation in Christ is enacted, and all receive food for eternal life. And there are the works of mercy. In being with the hungry and the thirsty, the destitute and the foreigner, the sick and the prisoner, the church meets Christ face-to-face. Thus at Pentecost the Holy Spirit clothes the church with power. To wear one's own size is to don this mantle, to exercise this power, to enjoy this blessing, confident that God has given the church everything it needs to discover, understand, and put to work the gifts it needs to fill the time between Christ's first coming and his second.

But there is more, much more. The third reason to wear our own size brings us to the most astonishing wonder of all. Essence becoming existence in Jesus isn't the whole of the story. God wants to share our limited, fragile, earthly life. But God doesn't simply want that, marvelous as it is. Essence empowering existence is not the end of the story either, breathtaking as that may be. There's more to it even than that. Jesus is fully human and fully divine—complete existence, utter essence. The Holy Spirit enables the church to discover and practice the life of essence in the midst of existence. Through Christ and the Spirit we realize what the Father's final purpose always was: *to bring us into essence*—into eternal truth. Jesus is God stretching out a hand and saying, Come into the essence of all things to be with me. In the painting of God and Adam on the ceiling of the Sistine Chapel in the Vatican in Rome, God's hand is stretched out in creation, almost touching Adam's hand. But the final purpose of creation is that God's hand stretches out a second time, in Jesus, *and invites us to become part of the very essence of all things*. That is the ultimate invitation. That is the indescribable offer. That is the unimaginable present. That is the inexpressible gift.

Having come to the pinnacle of the upside of humility—to wear our own size and inhabit the blessing bestowed upon us—it behooves us to glance again over the extent of the downside of humility—how precarious and wondrous is the path by which we have come to inherit that blessing. Grace comes to us as a story: a story in which much, perhaps most, could have been very different, indeed could have not been at all.

Recognize: had God not called Abraham, there would be no covenant. There would be a covenant of life, proclaimed in Noah, that never again would God destroy creation; but there would not be a covenant of a people, in which the story begins, a people at least as dear to God as God was ever to them. There would not be the notion of blessing, that this story was not for that people alone, but that in them, all peoples would find a blessing. Had God not sent Isaac, there would have been no way for that story to continue. Had God not sent the ram in the thicket when Isaac was bound as a living sacrifice, that story would have ended almost as soon as it had begun. Had Joseph's brothers succeeded in their purpose to kill him, there would have been no one to transform the agriculture of Egypt and provide for Israel in times of famine.

Had God not met Moses in the burning bush, there would have been no leader to guide Israel; there would have been only slavery. Had God not brought the Hebrews through the Red Sea, freedom would have died as soon as it had been born. Had God not sent manna, Israel would have starved in the wilderness. Had God not made the covenant of the law on Sinai, Israel would not have known who it was and what it was for and how to keep God's blessing. Had God not led Ruth through her faithfulness to her kinsman Boaz, there would have been no David. Had God not given Solomon riches, there would have been no Temple. Had God not spoken through Isaiah and Jeremiah, there would have been no vision in exile. Had God not worked through Cyrus and sent Ezra and Nehemiah, there would have been no return and no new Jerusalem. Had God not sent Esther to coincide with the threat to the Jews' existence, there would have been no Israel left at all.

Remember: had God not spoken to Mary and dwelt with us in Christ, we would not know we are children of a heavenly Father, made to be God's companions, empowered with the Holy Spirit. Had Joseph not escaped from Herod, there would have been no Jesus to call disciples, proclaim the kingdom, and open to us the heart of God. Had Christ not died in agony, we would not have discovered we mean everything to God. If Christ were not risen, we would not know that all of God's promises will come true and that our future is in God forever. If the Spirit had not come, we would not know the joy of this good news today. If God had not called Paul from his life as a persecutor to become an instrument of the Spirit, there would have been no gospel for the Gentiles. If we had not received the gift of baptism, we could not enjoy all these wonders through the church. Like Israel, we were made to be companions to God and a blessing to the creation. No more, and no less.

To be part of such a story is to discover what it means for your identity to be a gift, for your destiny to be beyond existence, for your past no longer to be a prison, and for the future to be your friend. All of this might not have been so. That all of this is so is not by chance or accident. It is blessing. And the most natural response to the discovery of blessing is praise. For praise is the recognition that the important things are not of our own doing but have been brought about by a will greater than our own, that that will is wholly good, and that that wholly good will does not just pervade existence, does not just prevail, but is indeed the essence of all things. And this will has, graciously, astonishingly, mysteriously, unimaginably, bent in our direction and swept us into its story, at indescribable cost to itself and with only marginal appreciation and endorsement from us. No amount of time could be sufficient to encompass or express such wondrous love as this.

Behold: you have been washed in the Jordan, anointed by the Spirit, crowned as a member of God's kingdom of priests, and clothed with power from on high. Wash one another's feet, be the servant and slave of all, make every act of your life a sacrament of love to others and a song of praise to God: for your existence is a miracle, and your redemption is amazing grace. And never cease from singing.

6

Be Faithful

Be a disciple. Strive to be what only you can be. Strive to want what everyone can have. To be a disciple means to be a person of wonder, of gratitude, and of discipline.

Be a person of wonder. Dwell with God. Walk with God. Immerse yourself in God's story. Open your existence to God's essence. Every day, discover more about God's goodness, truth, and beauty—in scripture, in history, in the world, in the universe, in happiness, in the face of tragedy, in abundant life, in the shadow of death: and call that praise. Recognize the ways your life has been but a poor reflection of that glory, forgetful of eternity, neglectful of blessing, contemptuous of judgment, greedy for gain, unmindful of others, unfaithful in love, cruel in ignoring pain, lazy in responding to need, slothful in praise, prompt in blame, absorbed in bitterness, slow to reconcile, restless in ingratitude: and call that confession. Acknowledge your neediness: your want of clothing, food, shelter, companionship, work; your longing for fulfillment, hope, faith, trust, joy, truth, fun, understanding, flourishing; your anxiety through intimidation, regret, ill-health, weakness, threat, poverty, danger, neighbor, enemy; your sense of another's need, amid tension, conflict, war, famine, earthquake, hurricane, hardship, bereavement, sickness, adversity; and the plight of the planet: and call that intercession. Name the ways your life might not have been, or might have been much more troubled, the gifts you've been given outwardly and inwardly, the heritage of faith, the constancy of love, and the hope of glory: and call that thanksgiving. Abide in the stillness such reflections yield.

Enjoy creation. No matter how sophisticated virtual forms of reality may become, they will never rival the real thing. Feel the sun on your forehead reflected off the snow, or the wind on your cheeks, hurtling in from the ocean. Let the water of the river run through your toes, or the pouring rain seep through your hair. Look deep into the wide blue yonder and contemplate the far horizon. Hear the chirrup of the tiny bird or the welcoming woof of the friendly dog. Behold the miracle of the rainbow, or shiver at the clap of thunder. Creation is seldom tame: beneath its sometimes gorgeous exterior lies menace and danger, occasionally in the jaw of a predator, more often in the enveloping arms of wave or the lurking trap of poison or sickness. Augustine says our lives are holy desire; and, like a cloth or leather purse stretched by the largeness of the coins it contains, so God stretches our soul by desire. "This is our life," he says, "to be exercised through desire." Likewise our souls are stretched by our apprehension of creation. Creation lifts our hearts by its extraordinariness and affirms our flesh by its ordinariness.

Befriend yourself. When Jesus says, "Love God, and your neighbor as yourself," he's referring to three loves (Luke 10:27). It's not that sacrificial renunciation of all good for the self in the name of serving the neighbor is detrimental to the self; it's that it's seldom genuinely helpful for the neighbor. Even when it doesn't distort mutuality, it still tends to nurture a roster of obligation and resentment. As with any friendship, take nothing for granted. Don't assume you can get to know yourself without spending time seeking to do so. Accept that your vices as well as your virtues are about a balance of innate inclination, practiced habit, good influence, and exercise of the will. Building trust in yourself is not inherently different from establishing trust with a friend or neighbor. In the marriage service the wife is asked, "Will you love him, comfort him, honor and protect him . . . ?" Such questions are well suited to relating to oneself. You are the first among the neighbors you are called to serve: therefore be kind—comfort, honor, and protect. The prophet Isaiah declares to Israel, "You are precious, honored, and loved" (Isaiah 43:4). There's little purpose waiting around for someone to say these words to you: sometimes you just have to say them to yourself.

Make friends who see and know and love the truth in you. A friendship is not a distraction, to take the mind off the dreary or burdensome, nor a diversion, to fill an idle minute with sixty seconds worth of exercise, company, or fun. A friend is not there to reaffirm your prejudices, justify your choices, dismantle your anxieties, amplify your self-regard, cloak you in assurance lest your world be challenged. A friend is a person with whom you gradually find the courage to tell the truth, about them and about you, in whom you name the poverty masked by wealth and the wealth masked by poverty, and whom you invite to name the same things in return. A friend is a companion who stands beside you as you face the most unpalatable things about your world, who doesn't run away or change the subject or make a joke or say, "It happened to me," but stares into your silence if there's nothing to be said. When a friend fails, you don't say, "That was unfair," or "You were robbed," or "You should protest," if the truth is "You weren't the best," or "You made a mistake of your own volition," or "You were taking the wrong course." You don't collude with a friend's fantasy of their own immortality, or their exaggerated despair over their own worthlessness; but you choose the right time to mention it, and you walk with them as they recalibrate their identity suddenly or by stages, and as they confront the behaviors that enhance their confusion. With a friend, it matters not if it be sunshine or rain, only that you are together, true, and existing in the light of the essence.

Honor your family. In some cases they are not what you would have chosen. In others they are what you chose, but would not have chosen had you known what you now know, or you rue that things have turned out as they have. Perhaps they are beyond what you could have desired or deserved. It could be you have no family, for good or ill, by choice, misfortune, or circumstance; maybe this is a deep sadness in your life, and you find other ways to develop the abiding interdependence, regular reliance, and mutual forbearance that family customarily supplies. If you have a spouse, and your spouse is also a friend, blessed are you; if not, your spouse is still family—and neighbor. If you have dependents, whether aging parents, vulnerable children, or relatives unable to live in their own strength, you learn the balance of joy and sorrow, struggle and reward, duty and devotion, comfort and hurt, responsibility and routine, that embodied existence encompasses. But remember: you were once a dependent, and most probably you will be so again; and you may well currently be so, in ways your longsuffering relatives are too merciful to name.

God, creation, self, friendship, family: these are wonders to enjoy. But there are also forms of thankfulness to cultivate.

Cultivate your talents. A talent appears at the intersection of your inherited characteristics; the environment and emphases of your upbringing; the challenges, needs, and opportunities of your world; and the particular purpose, urge, longing, and joy of your heart and soul. The pressure to earn a living and support a household may inhibit a talent or suppress it for a long time; a talent may long grow side by side with a means of deriving income, never becoming more than a hobby or secret indulgence; or a talent may remain little more than an eccentricity, a party piece, a road not traveled. Few and blessed are those who are able wholly to integrate their talent with the fiber of their days; and those who do (like an athlete or artist) sometimes find that should circumstances in themselves or the world change, and their talent is no longer so great or in so much demand, they have insufficient resources of identity or purpose on which to fall back. The mistake is to suppose one's talents are in short supply: it is absurd to think of there being just one, perhaps not yet discovered; talents need constant discovery, validation, cultivation, application, restoration, and recalibration. It's idle to think one can wake up being able to sing to perfection; it requires training, commitment, desire. Even then, making a living in so doing is unusual and precarious: but that doesn't mean it cannot bring delight to the bedside of a dying relative, inspiration to a classroom of neglected children, galvanization to an association of refugees longing to find their voice. It's fanciful to think that being able to whistle will bring financial reward or public acclaim; but to bring resilience to doleful prisoners of war, or to alert a search party to an ailing traveler lost in a jungle, it may be a gift second to none. To cultivate a talent is to express gratitude for being made the way you are—to see your own abundance rather than your scarcity, and to live in hope and trust that a moment will come when that talent will inspire, transform, or save.

Cultivate gratitude through work. Even if work does not fully or significantly engage your talent, even if its final purpose does not inspire or energize, even if its daily tasks are mundane and cumbersome, even if its conditions are trying and perhaps conflictual, even if your colleagues are not always supportive or congenial, work is still a gift. To earn money; to combine with others around a common goal; to meet people, see their gifts and vulnerabilities, offer kindness or practical assistance; to face challenges and find ways to overcome them; to put at least some of your physical and mental capacities to a constructive project—these are a cause for thankfulness.

Renew yourself through the formation and restoration of respectful and humble relationships. If you are an adult, find appropriate ways to spend time with a child. If you are young, discover how to make regular encounters with a person of senior years. If you have a disability, seek an intentional relationship with a person who knows nothing of the realities of your life, or is perhaps absorbed in the demands of their own. If you live in the country where you were raised, develop an understanding with a refugee or asylum seeker, or one who knows daily what it means to be a foreigner or stranger in a sometimes hostile culture. If you have a comfortable, secure home, be in conversation with a person who sleeps outside or is vulnerably housed. Don't assume your role is immediately to change the other person's reality, perception, opinions, or hardship: seek the interaction for your own sake, that you may more truly understand your own life and theirs, reconceive your own true wealth and your own true poverty, and, if sought and welcomed, walk with the other person as they make changes to their own experience of existence and address the constraints or pressures they face.

In addition to enjoying wonder and cultivating gratitude, practice discipline. Discipline has a negative side: it means developing the arts of resistance to aspects of culture that may tempt, flatter, comfort, and arouse, but may yet finally diminish, inhibit, stunt, and impoverish. If a small electrical device owns you, begin the day with a sacred time of refraining from reaching for it; have a whole day a week without being at its behest; identify conversations and moments it is never allowed to interrupt. If food, fashion, consumption, sport, celebrity, sex, appearance, money have altered from ways of expressing and enjoying health, fulfillment, leisure, or joy into forms of addiction, manipulation, imprisonment, or obsession, then discipline means developing a personal regime, sticking to limits, making yourself accountable to others, and investing in moderation. Discipline requires an effort of the will and a degree of self-love: but most of all it derives from a clear goal, a pearl beyond price, well worth making sacrifices for if it is finally to be attained. It must always be fundamentally saying a comprehensive yes, not just saying an arbitrary no.

Thus discipline is not just a cautionary approach, to avoid falling into the abyss: it is fundamental to flourishing. A prospector searching for gold will carefully sift through the dirt, gently discarding what should not be there and what serves no purpose, arriving finally at the small handfuls of soil in which the hint of a shiny substance appears. Likewise, as the waves of circumstance pound the shore of your life, leaving only scarce moments to scour the sand for glints of glory, rigorously examine yourself for what is gold and what simply glisters, that you may foster the lights of life, and set aside that which shrouds, drowns, or obscures it. Practice this habit weekly, daily, hourly, and you will become faithful.

7

Be One Body

Imagine being utterly one with God, completely reconciled with your neighbor, truly at peace with yourself, and wholly in harmony with creation. There's a word for those who seek such perfection: that word is "church." How and why church has come to mean a host of other things, many of them controlling, judgmental, posturing, and pretentious, is a long and complex story, much of it sad; but for all its missteps and misperceptions, church is the principal and definitive way essence takes form in existence, from the moment Jesus departed till the moment essence pervades existence and Jesus is all in all.

Be church. Live a life at one with God, reconciled with your neighbor, at peace with yourself, and in harmony with creation. Church means broadly three things. It refers, initially, to the body of Christ—the fully human, fully divine place where divinity and humanity meet, most explicitly in the incarnate Jesus, but derivatively in God's people, shaped by baptism, renewed by the Eucharist, empowered by the Holy Spirit, the place of reconciliation between heaven and earth, between essence and existence. It is not the full embodiment of Jesus Christ, nor is it the complete fulfillment on the last day—but in the meantime it is the physical and spiritual bearer of who Christ is and what it means and entails to be in full communion with him. Church means, second, the local manifestation of those seeking to inhabit this vision: church exists as a congregation of faithful people in which the pure Word of God is preached and the sacraments duly administered. It is a group of people doing their best to live with each other under God. Third, and less straightforwardly, church means those wider structures, institutions, relationships, and practicalities that enable the first two to flourish. Part of the paradox is that the attention of the world (and, to be fair, much of the church) tends to be drawn to the third dimension, thus often missing the most vital, vibrant, and thrilling facets of what church really means.

To be the body of Christ means to dwell in the freedom Christ brings—freedom from the prison of the past and from the fear of the future. It is to recognize that, through baptism, you have given up the claim that your individual body is the unit of creation, and allowed that body to be grafted in by the Holy Spirit to the true body, Christ's body, through which you participate in the life of God. You have given up your distinct identity, and you have yielded the final say on your own worth, purpose, and flourishing. So to participate in the body of Christ is to discover and reencounter your nature and destiny. It is hard to acknowledge that you no longer belong to yourself: it is to break the habits of a lifetime. Thus it is vital to be among a community in which such a recognition is universally held and assumed. In such a community you may learn to take the right things for granted. One of those things is that your life is set on a much greater canvas than your daily strivings, mundane desires, and perpetual squabbles might suggest. The way we discover that broader canvas is worship.

Worship is the name for the practice in which you most fully participate in the body; finding your place in God's story; being stripped of that which has become a barrier between you and God; naming your identity as forgiven, loved, and free; hearing God speak; being fed with the bread that never runs out; and being commissioned to go forth in love and peace. It is realigning your existence in the light of God's essence. Worship comes in many kinds. People may pray together informally by the need of the moment—sickness, sadness, crisis—or by habit. They may meet more formally to read and reflect on scripture, to praise, to confess, to intercede, to give thanks, to be silent. They may meet to share the sacraments of baptism and Eucharist that constitute the church. They may celebrate or commemorate specific occasions such as marriage or death, dedicating a beginning or marking an ending.

But to be church, rather than simply a person who combines with others to worship, means to participate in the daily practices of forming and restoring a local body of people and helping it to flourish in both the generic habits and the unique calling the Holy Spirit has given it as a church. And here the abiding theme is humility. The pitfalls of the church are two: people expect church to be an encounter with divinity and are impatient when that divinity is everywhere clothed in humanity, sometimes humanity of the most obstinate, unimaginative, and unattractive sort; or people are overwhelmed by the desires of their own imperfect humanity and attempt to use the capacity and potential of church to assert their personal needs for affirmation, security, or control— or, worse, exploit the opportunities of church to manipulate, take advantage of, or seriously harm those to whom they have privileged and trusted access. The first mistake is to forget how weak you are, and to expect others to be made of stronger fiber than you are yourself; the second mistake is to forget how good and beautiful and true is the enterprise in which you are engaged, and to reduce it to the most unworthy devices or desires of your own heart.

To participate in church means to belong to and seek fulfillment in a common project. Such a project involves many dimensions and stirs varied emotions. Some elements—such as practicing forgiveness and mutual accountability or seeking full integration of adults and children—seem unmistakably divine but feel humanly unachievable. Others—such as working out an annual budget or maintaining a building— may appear so human that it's hard to see through them to their divine source and goal. Others again—such as listening as a parent shares his difficulty in relating to his son, or helping a child find confidence to sing in front of a crowd—seem so small as to feel insignificant, but may be transformed by being part of a whole movement of people washing one another's feet in grand and unassuming ways. And then there are the disputes, divisions, and demands that are so disappointing, dispiriting, or discouraging that they paradoxically constitute the church by requiring disciples to depend on each other and hold fast to what is good when there can seem no convincing reason to carry on.

To belong to the wider structures, institutions, relationships, and practicalities of church is to recognize that communion means not just intimacy with God, not just a local congregation gathered as one, but also something less intense and less tangible: a body of people united around a faith, a person, a set of practices, or a form of words, unlikely to know one another well if at all, always likely to oppose unity to truth and pragmatism to hope, perpetually struggling to balance competing goods and to find understanding for one another's different stories and setbacks, opportunities and challenges. To exalt the body of Christ as intimate communion alone is to risk self-deception and self-indulgence. To exalt church as local congregation alone is to hazard an exclusive and narrow convergence of the like-minded. To seek the welfare of the whole is to experience the highs and lows of politics: sometimes it can be noble, visionary, and far-sighted; other times it can feel tawdry, cheap, and hollow.

For all, some of the time, and for some, most of the time, church means not just to participate but to initiate, promote, and lead. This is the difference between discipleship and ministry. In some traditions particular individuals are set apart to conduct roles that are considered integral to the church's life and indispensable to its flourishing. But such roles by no means exhaust the activities of ministry. Ministry means taking the initiative on any aspect that builds up the life of the body.

When it comes to being the body of Christ, seeking communion with the Father in Christ by the Spirit, particular practices and roles are especially evident. Preaching interprets the scriptures for today and seeks to bring disciples face-to-face with God.

Baptizing seeks to prepare people to become disciples through repentance and renunciation of the old life, washing by water and the Spirit, and clothing in the Spirit's gifts. Presiding at the Eucharist is about drawing the whole community into the mystery of Christ's death and resurrection. Pronouncing absolution publicly in worship or privately in pastoral care is a signal moment in reconciling a person to God. Corresponding practices may be formal or informal: a journey of forgiveness and/or healing is one in which many hands can play a part; training people for such roles involves many kinds of education and formation; fostering knowledge and inquiry and a culture of discernment and prayer is a task for a wide circle.

By contrast, enriching the life of a local congregation is not a restricted activity for a trained and commissioned few, but, ideally, a habitual part of community life for every disciple. As an army marches on its stomach, the vibrancy of a local congregation is largely dependent on the commitment and involvement of a wide range of volunteers. On one level this is a humble recognition of the variety and extent of the jobs that need to be done: keeping up the fabric of the building; counting and banking the money; offering hospitality and welcome; getting to know new members; addressing concerns about safeguarding the vulnerable, data protection, or health and safety; deepening fellowship; visiting the infirm—the list never ends. But on closer inspection there are three kinds of calling. There are those that require the self, just as you are, without skill, experience, depth of faith, or longevity in the community: rearranging chairs, serving coffee, making name cards. These have the danger of underusing a person's gifts, but have the advantage of accessibility and shared humility. There are those that draw upon skills and talents, whether professional or personal: preparing accounts, listening to the troubled. These have the danger of calcifying secular roles and hierarchies, but have the advantage of ensuring competence and experience. There are also roles that a person has never done, sought, or perhaps even imagined doing elsewhere or before, which require the Spirit to clothe them with what Paul calls spiritual gifts: laying hands on those who are sick, convening a gathering to wash feet. These may involve risk, but they can also bring about personal and communal transformation and disclose true vocation.

As to taking leadership in the wider church, like ordained ministry, this is perhaps not for everybody. The same diversity of self, skills, and Spirit applies: some things just need doing; some need doing by an experienced, perhaps qualified, person; and some may be points of unexpected gifts and calling. It means seeing the church as Christ sees it: not limited by time, not circumscribed by geographical space, not inhibited by its own shortcomings or clumsiness or failure, but led by the vision glorious and drawn into the mystery of grace.

Be willing to make your life transparent to others; be prepared to do humble and simple tasks; accept that your control, insistence on your own way, and right to be offended will all be in jeopardy; but at the same time be part of a movement following in Christ's footsteps, have your eyes opened to miracles of healing and transformation, and be ready to meet Christ face-to-face. In short, be one body: be church.

8

Be a Blessing

Be a blessing. Essence became existence in the form of Jesus Christ, existing as fully human from his essence as fully God. Through baptism, human beings respond to this gracious invitation to exist with God in Christ, and show their desire to be drawn through the Holy Spirit into the essence with God forever. The church is made up of those who have accepted this invitation, and who wish to be members of Christ's body in its ongoing earthly existence. But the life of existence isn't the eternity of essence; the church is not the kingdom. To be a blessing is not the same as to be church: it is to anticipate the life of the kingdom by modeling the ways God ultimately relates to the world and advancing the relations human beings will eternally have with one another. If being church is called ministry, advancing the kingdom is known as mission.

But it must still be humble. It is sadly not the case that church names perfect relations with God, self, others, and creation—in many cases, far from it. So when disciples or the church evangelize, campaign, advocate, or struggle to commend the life of the kingdom over the ways of the world, they do so knowing that there is no argument more persuasive than a good example, and that they have often failed to provide that good example. But even if they could hold up nothing but inspiring practice and stirring witness, they would still need to be humble, because there is a big difference between saying "This is a good way" and insisting "This is the only good way." The biggest danger in mission is that it becomes a form of self-assertion and self-promotion, all in the service of the advocates assuring themselves and proclaiming to others that they are superior, righteous, exemplary, and outstanding; thus "God" becomes no more than the clear blue water advocates put between themselves and those they wish to regard as beneath them. In such cases the world's deficits—oppression, inequality, despair, idolatry, disease—quickly become examples of what befalls the benighted world when it languishes without the gospel. But in truth all these shortcomings exist in the church also. So the question is, how to be a blessing yet still be humble?

There are two kinds of mission—that in which the primary goal is to give, impart, improve, and change, and that in which the intention is more to encounter, pay attention, receive, and grow. It is widely assumed that the first is noble while the second is selfish. But it's perhaps better to say that the first assumes one's own sufficiency and sees all the problems as lying elsewhere, whereas the second recognizes its own scarcity and humbly seeks wisdom, truth, and healing. Evangelism doesn't say, "My culture, intelligence, character, wealth, experience is superior to yours: now accept the story I tell and allow me to place you within it." Instead, it says, "Tell me how you see existence, purpose, and truth. Let me learn from you. Now will you let me describe what I hold fast to and what makes sense for me in the face of adversity, trials, suffering, and death?" After all, we don't want the outcome of our conversation to be the words, "I want to be you"; we want it to be, "Through you I have come to place my hope where it truly belongs and to have faith where once I knew only despair." Humanitarian aid doesn't say, "This is how a normal country works: we're going to give you these resources and this training and this technology until you can sort yourself out." It says, "We recognize that, while we have a great deal to learn from your country and culture, there remains an imbalance of wealth and stability between our two nations; show us where our assets can be helpful and teach us how to avoid being patronizing, colonial, or hypocritical." After all, we don't want the outcome of our actions to be the words, "You saved me"; we want it to be, "Through you I discovered resources in myself and my community I'd never drawn on before and will now be able to use in every future situation."

Be eager to learn and discover as much as to teach and transform. In the face of poverty, don't say, "You should do things more like me: use banks, create credit unions, deter loan sharks, develop cooperatives, establish support networks for microscale private enterprise, resist drugs and alcohol, budget carefully." Instead, say, "Tell me how you survive, help me understand how you get by. Tell me what it's like to go hungry so your children can eat. How are you hoping next year will be different from this year?" In the face of apparent injustice, don't say, "Your lowest standards don't conform to my highest standards, so I will protest as if I always kept my highest standards until you change and accord with them." Rather, say, "Help me understand how acting in this way makes your context safer, more productive, and more dignified, and how it encourages and motivates loyal, committed, energized people. May I share with you how this looks from the outside, and perhaps you could explain to me what's really going on from the inside?" In the face of troubling difference, don't say, "That's just wrong." Try, "I expect there are some things about my culture that you find disturbing or alarming. Please tell me about them, and then maybe I can share with you what I find difficult to comprehend about the way you do things."

Be spontaneous, but do not be culpably naïve: for your naïveté may disclose an arrogant assumption that your instant judgments outweigh the best efforts of many practitioners, or it may reveal a laziness that has no real interest in addressing a social challenge. You may find yourself in a city and be asked for money by a person who looks destitute. You probably knew in advance that you were going to be in that city. You were most likely aware that many city centers have a substantial number of people who ask for money. It takes no time to discover which agencies are working with those people. It is very easy to support those organizations financially. It is relatively easy to work through such agencies to volunteer material help or to spend time talking with and forming a genuine relationship with people in crisis. Such an agency will very probably know the individual who has approached you and have a much better understanding of their needs than you could form on an instant impression. Being humble means recognizing how real change comes about in a person's circumstances and life, and aligning yourself with those who spend their whole time working with people to help them find their own way out of poverty—not proffering a coin to assuage your guilt and avoid a person's pitiful or angry gaze.

Understand how power works to make change. When things are wrong, the causes may be misfortune, neglect, or ill will. If the reason is wholly or largely neglect, the answer may well be a campaign to ensure office-holders are held to account, are put under pressure to do what they had every obligation to do, or are replaced with people who will. Such a campaign is best led by those who hold authority, but they may need to be encouraged, informed, and hastened by those most aware of the damage caused, and it can take work to highlight an issue and present it in the public sphere in a way that shows a clear problem and a considered response that doesn't simply create further problems. If the reason is ill will, and persuasion has failed, a more adversarial approach may be called for, perhaps involving public exposure, even ridicule, through various media, and potentially a process involving law enforcement and the justice system. But when the reason is misfortune, such measures are inappropriate, and what is required is collective action at all levels, with each concerned person using their discrete skills, experience, network, and sphere of influence in a genuine team effort. All of these examples affirm the significance of organizing. Organizing means coming to understand each stakeholder's interests, building a movement with small successes leading to growing confidence to address greater challenges, and forming a coalition that sees common cause for a limited period around public good. Again, be humble: you aren't necessarily the best judge of precisely what's wrong or exactly how things should be or ideally how to get from one to the other; but if you are prepared to relax your control, your defended identity, your prerogative about every detail, and your insistence on getting the credit, then remarkable things can be done.

Look deep into your tradition for models of social hope and collective action. In the gospels Jesus spends a very long time coming to know, understand, and share the culture and plight of his people. He makes a public gesture of humility in being baptized, then faces up to the temptations of the role he is taking on. He gathers together, trains, and empowers a group of followers. Through explicit instruction and public gestures, he portrays the new reality he has been advocating. In going to Jerusalem he faces the cost of the change he seeks. In all these ways he sets a path to follow. The New Testament in general perceives the key agenda for the world as one of reconciliation. It offers a host of practices—apology, repentance, confession, penance, forgiveness, healing—each of which has a role to play in reuniting us with God, ourselves, one another, and creation. The key is to realize that all is reconciliation: there is no "other thing" to be getting on with; there is simply a choice between sticking with an existing process or diverting to another one whose challenges seem lighter and whose rewards seem closer. Evangelism isn't an alternative to or a consequence of or a precursor to reconciliation, but a subset of it. Difference, tension, conflict, and war are all invitations to a process of reconciliation, which will continue (or be ignored or subverted) until kingdom come. To be in the process is to be oriented toward the kingdom. But to be committed to reconciliation is to recognize with humility how deeply, and no doubt unconsciously, you are part of the problem, and to be genuinely willing to change, even at great cost.

In all your sophistication and analysis and strategy-setting and social awareness, never forget the goal of all change: truthful and trusting face-to-face personal relations in which people discover who they are and the gift they are to one another, addressing the most painful realities in their lives and sharing their greatest joys. Deprivation is grievous if it makes this impossible; but prosperity is unworthy if it makes it no more likely. Injustice is abhorrent if it undermines this or hinders it; but vindication is not healing, success, or transformation if it does not facilitate or enable it. Suffering is miserable if it inhibits being with one another; but alleviation is incomplete if it doesn't include deeper bonds of understanding and grace. Artistic talent, sporting prowess, academic achievement, medical accomplishment, professional excellence, and resilience in the face of physical, economic, or circumstantial adversity are all admirable qualities; but they are inadequate if they do not yield genuine, profound, tender, abiding relationships of truthful encounter and sustained mercy.

For this is the heart of it all. In humility we accept that we are tiny, pointless, transient specks in the inconceivable enormity of space-time existence. But in grace we discover that the personal quality of essence, which we call God, has chosen to enter existence, and to become one of us, because of a primordial desire to be with us, in tender, understanding, gentle, humble relationship with us—and that that was the reason for existence in the first place. But not just this: we discover also that this being with, which we call Jesus, sets forth a capacity to live in this relationship henceforth, a capacity we call the Holy Spirit; and that the ultimate purpose is for God not just to share existence with us, but to draw us finally into essence and dwell with us forever, even when all existence has passed away. And so every time we form, establish, restore, and deepen tender, understanding, gentle, humble relationship with one another, we imitate and anticipate the way God seeks to be with us, and glimpse the glory of eternity. Which could make us entitled and self-important. Yet we realize it could so easily not be so: and certainly would not be so if our deserts were taken into account. And even now we struggle to comprehend the magnificence of what we are being offered; and our lives inadequately represent those to whom has been extended such an astonishing gift. And so, as ones unworthy, unprepared, and largely incapable of comprehending whence we came and whither we are going, we remain, until the last day, truly, deeply humble: and thus become a blessing.

Wonderings

Wonderings are not questions. They do not end with a question mark. They are a form of exploration that is neither a statement nor a question nor a request nor an order. They are an invitation to ponder, dwell, and linger. I would usually divide these wonderings into two kinds. "Tell me about" would be the ones that invited a story about the past. "I wonder" would be the ones that invited speculation about the unknown or the future. Since these wonderings are designed for individual reflection as well as group study, I have rendered them all as "I wonder."

Chapter 1

I wonder which is more mysterious—that there is existence, or that there is essence.

I wonder whether all truth is a balance between chance and love.

I wonder whether love is attentive patience.

I wonder what it feels like to realize we depend.

I wonder what it means to you to honor your parents.

Chapter 2

I wonder who else you think of when you hear the words, "You have no idea how many people it takes to keep that man in poverty."

I wonder how many people it takes to keep each one of us.

I wonder if you ever achieved something impossible with a great team, or failed to achieve something easy with a poor one.

"Gratitude is the moment we turn from seeing dependence as a burden and begin to see it as a gift." I wonder what these words mean to you.

I wonder how your life looks when viewed backwards from the deathbed.

Chapter 3

I wonder whether you live your life as a party designed to distract yourself from the truth.

I wonder what the stars tell you.

I wonder whether anyone really makes a difference.

I wonder what it means to you to be (or to wear) your own size.

I wonder what the story of the wolves of Yellowstone National Park means about your embeddedness in the world.

Chapter 4

I wonder which of the nine fruits of the Spirit is most nearly about you.

"Kindness is treating those outside the circle as if they were in the circle." I wonder if anyone has ever been kind to you.

"Our first gift is presence and attention." I wonder whether you have been on the receiving end of such gifts.

I wonder if you have discovered that "the heart has its reasons the reason knows not of."

I wonder if you have ever been hasty with your horror, fury, or scorn.

Chapter 5

I wonder whether there is a story in your family or nation that demands to take precedence over other stories.

I wonder what it meant for essence to become existence.

I wonder what it might mean for you to be drawn from existence into essence.

I wonder whether you feel you are in the middle of a great story, or toward the end or the beginning.

I wonder what it might mean to you to be a person of praise.

Chapter 6

I wonder what enjoying creation means to you.

I wonder what it means to comfort, honor, and protect yourself.

I wonder if you have a friend who "stands beside you as you face the most unpalatable things about your world."

"To cultivate a talent is to express gratitude for being made the way you are": I wonder what that means to you.

I wonder what you have discovered about discipline always being fundamentally a saying yes, not just a saying no.

Chapter 7

I wonder how it feels to read the words "church is the principal and definitive way essence takes form in existence."

I wonder which of the three understandings of church most resembles your experience and perception.

I wonder whether it is hard to acknowledge that you no longer belong to yourself.

I wonder which of the two pitfalls of church most resonates with you.

I wonder with which form of ministry—self, skills, or Spirit—you most readily identify.

Chapter 8

"There is no argument more persuasive than a good example." I wonder if you have ever seen a good example of Christianity.

I wonder whether you have ever seen a kind of mission that has become a form of self-assertion and self-promotion.

I wonder what it would be like if all mission were a humble request to discover and to grow.

I wonder how much naïveté is a disguised form of arrogance.

"Every time we form, establish, restore, and deepen tender, understanding, gentle, humble relationship with one another, we imitate and anticipate the way God seeks to be with us." I wonder if this is so for you.

Notes

1. In the film *Merry Christmas, Mr. Lawrence*, the prison commander, Captain Yonoi, asks the prisoner, Major Jack Celliers, "Do you know who I am?" Celliers insolently, but poignantly, replies, "No. Do you?" and is rewarded with a sound beating. But the question abides.

2. The story of the wolves' return to Yellowstone is told in "How Wolves Change Rivers," narrated by George Monbiot, www.youtube.com/watch?v=ysa5OBhXz-Q.